Touching The Headstone

– *Stride* –

TOUCHING THE HEADSTONE
Simon Perchik

TOUCHING THE HEADSTONE
First edition 2000
© 2000 Simon Perchik
All rights reserved
ISBN 1 900152 14 2
Cover design by Neil Annat

Acknowledgements
American Writing, Art/Life, Bitter Oleander, Black Warrior Review,
Boulevard, Chelsea, Colorado Review, Confluence, Context South,
Denver Quarterly, Descant, Dirigible, Free Lunch, Hawaii Review,
(The) Journal, Kerf, Kinesis, Manoa, Massachusetts Review,
New Letters, Nexus, Northwest Review, Ohio Review, Osiris,
Painted Bride Quarterly, Partisan Review, Pavement Saw,
Pembroke Magazine, Pequod, Peregrine, Phase & Cycle,
Pikeville Review, Plum Review, Poet Lore, Poetic Page,
Puerto del Sol, Quarry Review, Racs, Reed Magazine,
River King, Shearsman, Small Pond, So To Speak,
South Dakota Review, Southern Humanities Review,
Sun Dog, Takahe, Talus and Scree, Tantra, Tightrope,
Underground, University of Windsor Review,
Verse, World's Best Poetry, Yefief.

Published by
Stride Publications
11 Sylvan Road, Exeter
Devon EX4 6EW
England

Touching The Headstone

To James L. Weil, Edward Butscher, and Anslem Parlatore
for their poetry and friendship; to Edward Weston whose
photographs inspired this work; to the owners, employees and
customers of Fierro's Pizzeria where these poems were written.

For Casey, Vaughn, Marieke and Katherine.

•

It's easy to grow tall, you pee
against a tree and the faintest sound
grinding the sky into puddles, rain
oceans! warmed by relentless waves
tied, and with the same split second
untied, heated till the turbulence
and along the bark you feel a sea wind
cooling the branch already nursing
from the same knot that cradled
its first born leaf and thirst

– it's simple, you begin to hate the house
the doors, the rooms and the sun too
off on its own, never again allowed
in the ground – you make a sea
to cover your arms and lifting branches
becomes easier – you teach the roots
to float and the needle-sharp stars
you will feel even when your fingers
let go and the sky is suddenly dark
teeming with icy peaks
weightless, taking you with them.

•

Marieke will sense the heft
knot each lace the way all mothers
still give birth always to twins

– she likes the bows
lets them loosen, wider and wider
for feathers, ties her ankles

till they overflow, begin to gust
and each step closer to the sun
– she will wax these shoes

bathing them as if the sun
could be encouraged, would jump
at night :a second sky

filled with a new light
still without footprints
and the sun reaching up

for one heel, a blister
just starting, already waves
and shoreline, each tiny shoe washed
for more wingspeed and tighter.

●

It's simple, you stretch the cloud, sparks
even in winter and inside the fuselage
a ladder, rung over rung reaching out

for sunlight and the smoke is heated
first without water – a blossom
a covering, a shadow floating

under your arms – you spread the flames
the way propellers once warmed the sky
with feathers, stepping stones, lift off

and the headwind through which all bedrock
flows, one fire holding a place
for the other, the slow, climbing turn

that hollows even brick – it's easy, grow
a plume from a stick broken open
give it the leaves

no one needs now and as they scatter
rake in the air where rain has fallen
and the crash taking root inside ashes

that reek from bones :millstones
splashing their huge wings
wheels down for the landing.

●

•

It's when you sweat that a raft
spreading out as if your belly
and the small candle inside
tries to set the sky on fire
– slow, so your mouth
will stink from salt and plankton

– you wait till noon, mow the lawn
half sea, half wooden table
half when you swallow the cold beer
your breath fills with coastline
with waves and the sunlight
no longer thirsty, this time

afraid – it's when you open your jaws
let them float over the chipped tooth
the missing finger, the thunderheads
and your skin drains, keeps out the cold

– you bathe this heat into rows
shirt sleeves rolled, elbows bare
where the bones sniff for air
for dirt and the long dive back

– from miles away you can hear
one sea calling another, lost
– you drink the stones to finish.

●

This time the splinter, wedged
the way even a board fights back
– warpaint! your thumb tipped

with peroxide and just above the ridge
falling birds, falling branches, your finger
already infected, changing colors

is swollen with rivers as if one arm
weighs more and slowly the poison
sifts for dirt, soaks in

beginning to sting where your finger
caresses a hinge, a lid, a kiss
and this needle-thin paint

a deadly brown, a suddenness
that takes down even moonlight
once it touches the skin and dries.

•

And the headwind still visible
charred the way you use both hands
to steady this grill, bank its grate

into some battered, climbing turn
as if this fire could untangle
replace the sky with another sky

while your eyes burn to the ground
– your breath nurses the smoke higher
smells from rust and engine oil

and one arm under your heart, the other
rebuilt with gristle and bone and glue :ashes
used over and over for screaming.

●

To start the limp you lace
the way all mothers remember
and the warm, dark rivergrass
where birds still nest

– you tie one shoe tighter
till its shell cracks open
and under each fingernail the pieces
smell from damp mud, broken reeds
riverside – the bow stays wet

as if each egg learned long ago
to cling without flying away
– with each step feathers everywhere
dragged while the other shoe

is washed in bronze, carries you off
for later – you squeeze one foot
so the other will harden, grow
wingtips for its powerful dive

towards stone and you walk forever
high up on your toes, spreading out
the limp all shells hear breaking apart
crumbling into footsteps

and shoreline, creaking
as if some cradle would suddenly
be heard in the birds all night
who sing to it, followed slowly
by mountainsides and drought.

Half luck but still you need a booth
a gate, and the throughway rising
as if your random throw already knows

the sacred spot is underground, you steer
and the car brings down the tunnel walls
– a great fireball and for the third time

you phone, claiming credit, half toss
half revenge, half all those other drivers
screaming, boiled alive in the light

inside the light till nothing floats
except the cry each child learns
for its first breath

still, you need a well, a basket
filled with riversides and the Earth
open again and overflowing.

＊

Nobody said it was easy
– hanging knives, invisible yet
juggled as if your arms
don't belong to you, tossed
one behind the other
and overhead that featherless river

– no one sees you circle the airport
careful not to cut yourself
adjusting for turbulence, windshear
and on all sides the waterfall.

Casey, thirst can help with this
keep track and while the sky is stirred
drink, it cures forgetfulness
– you can retrace those waters
every mother heats with just her arms
and lullabies – practice! those blades
are already timed, holding your palm
face up, listening for stars
as they reach near the surface.

•

While overhead the camera
circles the way rock is sweetened
begins to melt, gradually the crater

cracks though it's June and your cup
somewhere alongside
– all night, every night

you scan for news about disaster
sit too close as if the screen
would show the altitude, adjust

for crosswind and the dented kettle
that still needs repairs, maintenance
– the TV crews feeling their way

through lava and mountainside
– you never reach the controls
never shut down the set

let it idle, filling this room, the Earth
pouring out your lips and skies
you once sang from your shoulders.

●

There's still some driftwood :my throat
half underwater, half floating
bloated, beginning to gel

and between my lips
useless tides, rotting fishtails, kisses
– all that survived is spit

kept warm as if it remembers
a time – relentless shells: my teeth
once lips and now serrated

except these two, strays
still watersoaked, unable to gnaw
through the seaweed I come here

to feed on till there's no flesh left
and I cling to table legs, the chairs
facing each other, just as it used to be.

•

And glue each feather closer
though when you pull back a deep breath
a nest shrieks – this makeshift arrow

clawing your fingers open for lift off
– you aim dead center and the sun
slowly the way a lid already covers one eye

while the other pinpoints the deluge
– carefully, you open the bow
into umpteen zillion years still smelling

from salt and lift off
– you will blame
the sky should be bigger

but who you going to believe, me
or these feathers falling off
as if they wanted to spread lower

shake from the sea floor
the sun overflowing with sea gulls
pouring out its darkness and oceans.

•

It's the limp, an invisible heel
– you practice the way all stragglers forget
glass cures – off and on, on

and the village cheers how easily it fits
matches and carried house to house
on horseback – it's the one eye

half late, half stomping the new glasses
and the scratches you can't see through
though it's a bedtime story

a you-want-it, you-got-it grandmother
a wand lowered over your eyes
your beautiful nose, your ears

– even asleep you will listen
for that glass, sometimes
near a clock, sometimes

a faint footstep rushing home
and already you can count to 10
the fingers in your shattered hands.

•

To cover the table you use two sacks
one for collecting stones, one kept empty
and air rising the way bread is baked

– you cool your mouth with stone
so no one hears you toss back your head
half mouth, half blood spinning down

– you can't eat like that! cutting slices
just to look at a sky not yet morning
though one glove is always heavier

and the crumbs cling to your fingers
to this empty light and table – you sit
as if another slice might make the difference

two lips would grow from your own
quietly into place
clot this darkness and crust.

●

You dig the way this urn
brushes against what once was sunlight
– with just a spoon feed it rains
flickering from far off

stirring the dirt by instinct
and this stove half smoke
half charred, half great oceans
circling down for their first evening.

You pour for the updraft
the side to side to someone else
who is thirsty, cold and water
was all there was, was facing you
in the dark without these stars
without your hands around it

– you fill this cup
with a shovel: a bell
overflowing and your teeth
scorched, crusted from topsoil
from one night more
falling through your throat.

•

The one wrestler empty handed
and though this crowd already feels
the seabreeze, the grappling tides
still shaping – Vaughn can't wait

pounces, sure the sun is winded
– he closes his eyes so it makes sense
to trip and even asleep the oceans
go wild, cheering him on – what he hears

is that blinding cliff: the sun
on its feet again, exhausted
can be caught and dives the way nights
reach under for leverage, set up
the spin – the sun can't get a hold

splashing against one night to the next
and another sea born weeping
begins to breathe, kept warm in his sleeve
and his fall bleeding into place.

•

You don't feel the wallop
though every branch takes revenge
freezes the dirt till every leaf
is brought back green again – this bat

uproots as if a river once
and between your tiny fingers
reaches down to drink a rain
not yet smelling from stone
and the burnt grass overhead

– your hands are filled with stones
kept dark in a cardboard box, each piece
opened till it fits exactly, spreads out
into a sky made whole again
and the thin, blue flower you hold up
waiting to catch another.

It's just a bat-and-ball game
– your hands reaching under
a drop-by-drop mountainside
that should be back in place by now

– both hands cupped and this drizzle
falling the way winter
finds these stones for you, sorts
and from each evening another star
turns black, evens things out
and the days too are breaking in
through the ice.

•

You shower the way a prisoner
is given the pressed suit, a ticket home
– you soak the faucets

to unlock some gate half iron
half both your wrists reaching around
for that smallbone smell

from your legs just learning to walk
and the sun who has not named you yet
giving you another chance.

You will wrap the towel
so you can tell time by the knot
a new tie makes, folded into the Earth

holding it down while the evening
is sent back as waterfall
and overhead its huge millwheel

covering you with handfuls
and dirt ground fresh
for your shoes and shirt and rain.

•

The tree has no heat left, and there
its leaves shivering the way stars
are melted down before they freeze
kept dry, adrift on wood
that can't warm anyone
and under your fingernail, charred
icing over – you point out

where on the sky the garden tools
are rusting and every night
it's the same, there
the handheld radio full throttle
and in the other a chainsaw.

You are listening for static
give your fleecelined gloves
the names animals are called
and fish and there the ramp
the wing, the tail, the oil leaks
and between the landing lights
the promise, by tomorrow night

another shed, alongside
as if more logs could end the rain
with just sawdust and the radio louder

closer – you stack logs
the way rain is brought
from further than these stars
from some fire and you track the place
returning drop by drop
with your hands unable to open.

•

Even your stone is rotting
and this shallow pond dug under you
helps those migrating tides
listen for moonlight, and closer seas.

You already reek from sand
from beachgrass growing mold
half green, half gray, half blur.

You must be an old man by now
on shore, pushing off
and the relentless nights
that remember this place
are harvesting just one stone

star by star till all that's left
is scratched, leaking and you drink
from a stone going bad
before it could become a waterfall

and upstream the rapids, each rock
pressing under another rock
the way mountain ranges are lifted

one by one and from out the Earth
are slowly floating over it
and then the others.

Don't even think about it!
Fudge one syllable or forget
– you'll mistake the way

– in Marieke's crib every word
is filled with forests
ferocious wolves, bears

and half asleep why should she
as if it's just a story
and slipshod work believable.

Act surprised you've lost track
– praise is how she makes corrections
crosswinds 10 to 20 from the west

ceiling zero, rains
– she knows these trees
by heart, that there's always

the clearing and sunlight
where it's safe to sleep, where
the fairy mother, the other

slipper or was that further back
– you can't hold on, the page
is breaking apart – more altitude

and she's already on your shoulders
pointing where to turn, one way
or the other or again tonight

closer to the window you'll try
not to frighten her
and the broken glass she thinks

is part story, part where she takes over
and you say you can't see
need more light, more room, more candy.

•

And your upper jaw
though no one sees
how the silk, full blown

half white, half red
half these tiny mushrooms
heating in milk

the way decaying trees
still give birth
get that second chance

and the stench become again
the yell for jumping clear
– you're used to Campbell's Soups

lift each lid as if the dead
with just half water, the spoon
half throttle, filled

with headwinds: from this waterfall
– it is this can broken apart, this mouth
that remembers, can't close

and these returning planes
by the handfuls, gathered
from the rotting skies, the rotting dirt.

●

You are dead for hours, years
and every morning, first
I soap their backs, one hand

closes slowly into the other
– you are cleaned always twice
always a sink smelling from pine

and bed sores, your leg
dangling and drop by drop
enters my hands the way every window

still shuts out the air
– it's this first-thing-in-the-morning
thing I do because – don't laugh

– I must touch you in my sleep
or something that sounded like two mourners
behind you, along side

and even these faucets look thirsty
need more water from this room
this shallow, small, dark where you

are throwing off your clothes
to bathe alone, in emptiness
in nothing left to wish for

except one hand pressing against your stone
squeezing it and the other already smooth
filling with your lips and rain.

°

It could be the birdbath
caressed and the Earth
still melting into oceans, lakes

– could be the ice forgets
surfaces where I trace your lips
sip from the sharp stone

all winter chipping off feathers
splashing and my palms
again the cradle birds know

is heated with stones
waiting too – could be this
the smooth, humming one

rising through kisses and the ice
already singing to its shoreline
– could be you hear each half

closing in: one stone
cracking open the sun, the others
full length, over you.

·

It's leaking so don't brush
don't shave, abandon your cheeks
on jutting weeds and rock

– drop by bloodshot drop this faucet
lifts from the bottom sand
the way some artist will abstract

till nothing's left from the bridge
except the unbearable rain
and one arm filled with numbness

so you dead can return, mouth open
– a lilting gibberish
you don't recognize

is trembling on your lips and more lips
– don't stop this dripping, go
for zero, the worn down

from constant tightening one death
to another – fill this sink
with cures, hammers, more girders

relentless words, ecstasy
that will weigh enough
to bend your arms together.

●

At least a dozen times
– you watch the hole, its front paws
huddled while the ones behind

can't run fast enough, kick downwind
as if lift off was not important
to its bone – your jaws closed

it's always the same half a handful
tossed over one shoulder
and you pat the dog's legs

as if you were flicking pages
filling in where the sky forgets
– with just one hand and your knees

torn open from loosening more dirt
letting it float and overhead
a summer breeze taking you by the arm

still falling from your shoulder, the other
wider and wider, smoothing the ground
between feathers, frozen peaks

that no longer bark – you drag the bone
to one more valley, started minutes ago
and all those valleys.

•

The table too has come to stay
though each morning its crust
is ground for flour, sifted, stones
unfolding into arms, legs, breasts

– with each mouthful more crumbs
becoming mulch, branches, roots, leaves
– you don't need the sun, it's enough
the kitchen has grown around you :mountains

half marrow, half that burnt taste
all dirt and this soft tablecloth
pulled closer to your lips
by the handfuls – you too

are lifted with that same bread
every rain gathers into hours, years
– are cooled, allowed to snow: each slice
left uncovered, expecting you.

•

Without a bubble the lake
icing over, that black cat
from nowhere and somebody drowns
always at night, with lightning

– in these movies the screen stays dry
though it's still dangerous
skating so close, the markers shaped
as if the hag was somehow changed

into a deep breath holding on
for hours – by summer
there are no forests, the drowned
become the favorite child, fed

nothing but that one-breath-more
its only joy, on horseback
too weak to reach and the shore
expanding the way all ice

drains to redeem the world
– you watch how it ends, the broom
half straw, half dimmer and dimmer
rubbing just one arm and nobody's darling.

·

And under the blindfold this kite
half luck, half breathing
– it's just a party game

a wide climbing turn
as if the sky too would be opened
and you can tell by the rejoicing

how close you are – even in the dark
the tail pinned so the dead
suddenly whole, are put back

the way stars will strike one shoe
while the other wanders off
pokes from the dirt the huge ears

the hooves, the plow – you can't see
– the ground too is beginning to gust
has found a place closer

is entering, already weightless, the updraft
colder than string and lifting
one heel tighter, one always slack.

•

She uses only the generic, in time
push will be the last resort
and in its place the bloodstains
where the swing came back ravenous

– for now it's enough and she holds on
the way ice covered streams are drained
with spawning stones :her language
just starting out, needs sunlight

and lift, headwinds to bleach her cheeks
till you make out the word for where
there are no trees and under her wings
clouds empty and fill – two ropes

one swollen from the sound
for moonlight over her shoulders
– she yells *push* and you hear the avalanche
the trembling kiss taken from her mouth

though her lips are closed
not yet feathers, already flying
– the finishing touches: each dive and climb
strikes the air for more air

till her throat fills with the height
that will forget the sudden turn
the branch thrown off course
and one rope still falling back, lifeless.

•

Even this phone, swollen the way all mothers
still hear the ocean just before sunrise
– in the dark you lift the receiver

and with both arms as if two whales
are swaying for miles and miles, calling
while for hours you listen for waves

not sure which is half the world away
– at this depth all voices become songs
coming closer, still warm from her breasts

– before you take hold the phone
rub it, soften the water, let it rise
to your shoulder, your throat

is something else, at most a few cries
– listen till some tiny brook
reaches your ear and you are carried down

though your voice is not stone
– before you say hello! be careful you're
already shoreline: the shallow climb

when one wave, then another alongside
half foam, half saliva, half asleep
and you will lift your arms from the bottom sand

whose cry you still hear as far away
as moonlight splashing towards your breath
your lips and the unbroken dial tone.

•

Your left shoe is always colder, the sun
rising as moonlight and the slow, wide turn
tightens till one cracks open, the other
keeps its shine as if each moon
would drift forever on that darkness
the sun takes to its grave – a limp

always to the left, half shoe
half that same leather jacket
drenched where the ice melted
never reached – inside just one ankle
the marrow is still in flames
and you drag its bones the way streams
break apart, circling deeper and deeper
into the center where the Earth
tries to put out the fire – rusted, weather-beaten

one shoe who has no memory
is falling back in smoke, in darkness
the cold and these stars: each footstep
born already grieving, one finally behind the other.

•

Even without their feathers, kisses
all that's left though your lips
somehow remember the sunlit ravines, open
the way mourners still warm their hands
single file, let the silence
carry them up, who know
where in the ground each breath
is heated, lifted and your throat made soft

– whispers are what you want, you listen
for the returning stones, for clouds, agree
to distances – you wait for mist
still damp from some lifeless sea
weightless below its eyes
that can barely see the rain
– you open your lips and the drizzle
has this echo, drink
from a sky carved from stone
a small stone who loves you.

●

This handle slopes the way each fountain
still remembers it was once a sun
a great arm towering and over the Earth
its shadow becomes too heavy
oozes along the ground – you pump

just for the darkness
carry it up by the mouthfuls
by the stones that can't move anymore
or change color, or open

to attract the morning
before it touches the dirt
or harden – you drink with your shoulders
almost in flames, almost
holding back the sun
and over the cup your fingers
tighten into the slow, wide turn
that no longer climbs by itself – one arm
heavier, filled with heartbeats
and the emptiness alongside.

•

You almost drown and what's left
from an abandoned temple wall
– on one knee carefully break loose
that shadow the dead restore
with more room, more air

– you build a trench for clams
brought back the way clouds have learned
to grasp your shoulders for water

and clam by far off clam
trembling, fitted into bottom sand
into a shell already gray and your hands
never clasp, never dry or open again.

•

You try to make sense, the radiator
won't cool though its slender hose
is already covered with winter

layer on layer – you guess
it's the windshield, every breeze
overheats and under the tinted glass

the smoke rises a dark blue
– for a split second the sky
holds to the surface

and from the distance some priest
measures the ram led over to the greasy pit
where the mechanic snaps a cold tool

on ancient rivers and your throat.
It snows with new parts, your lips
almost human, almost one finger

pressed against the still sharp key
– it shakes with a climb
that is not a bird, not the sun

or the scent from a graceful turn
about to say something slowly
barely flesh – it starts when the hood
closes though no one is inside or weeping.

•

This tray and the stench
half flesh, half bone – a were-stone
part mountainside, part airborne
though the mourners will say
it's for some bird
who might be cold
or theirs or incense: your breath
lifeless from this headstone
except when at night the sun
is filled from valleys
that are not feathers

– no, this is not the last kiss
though you devour these stones
as if moonlight is not enough
while it hardens on your lips
eats away at the Earth
at your mouth and this lettering
almost tender, outstretched, calm.

•

Still tries and each winter
a skim rushing to surface
– escape is possible, this time
I add salt till the egg
boils the way stars remember
how to open in the cold

and leave – it takes patience
– the shell cracks just so
lights up as if all those years
the sun was packed in ice
and never forgot, every year
more snow – it takes snow

and practice, a seabird not yet born
though its enormous wings
are already half waves
half broken apart – it becomes a game

splashing water till the air inside
is freed, sputters and the rickety climb
– a deadly ritual: this iron pot
at exactly 30,000 feet will break apart
half flak, half sunlight flickering

– it takes sea water, stirred
till each breath becomes a cooling headwind
lifts one arm across the other
and over this rusting stove more snow.

●

And though my lips are harmless now
this envelope is too tight, my jaw
fitted for the freezing rain

and glue holding down a stamp
that is not snow or another front
closing in behind the drop in pressure

– you will open it with a knife
expecting danger, teeth but inside
there's a letter folded as if rain

is nothing but your hand tightened
over mine – you will open it
the way ice drifts, breaks apart

from emptiness though the letter
says nothing about wolves
or moonlight howling to remember

– I send you the cage where my lips
tangled, bareheaded, rancid
– I send you the bandage. Open it!

●

Even in the womb these leaves
have their father's thirst, the tree
coming here to die

lowers its still warm breasts
– between the branches each leaf
draws its first breath

from water, splashes
and in the shallow light
that is not the sky – every Fall

half exhausted, half headwaters
half mountainside and the sun
slinking off to cool

– you don't burn the usual pile
– you rake a narrow stream
a riversong to open sea, mouth open

louder and louder till the yard
spreads out into a great wing
and over the abandoned roots

more darkness, a motionless pole
and in your palms a lullaby
held out for rain and burial.

•

Shameless! you rush one finger
and under the snow lift this rock
– it has nothing to do with the casket
though the dead tell time with stone.

One hand is always weighted
so when your other arm rises
it's learning one from one
just by tracing it, caressing

one letter, ...another, louder, louder
– you can't wait for the E
almost touching the headstone
wrapped tightly around you

all these years reaching up
though all you need is one
or just a part or a fingernail
– the snow is coldest where the lettering

huddles to one side the way mourners
reach in back for jetties
and this tiny rock placed against the snow
to stave off continents – you need the snow

to get a better grip, a pendulum
pointing always toward the dead
as when some great sea is struck
by a rock that is not moonlight

and you hear one, ...deeper and where
the devouring zero is listening
even without the schoolroom bell
or footsteps standing in line.

•

It's just a roof: the jacket
is not supposed to last
and though the collar lines up

you come here to jump head first
into a wind that is not a runway
or a bridge over the Hudson

held close by broken rakes
mower parts, the plywood weatherbeaten
– a shed made famous for eluding death

and high enough to lure
these rickety ladders, frayed rope
the worn-out-not-yet-dead garden tools

who undo great heights
though the zipper doesn't climb anymore
rusts the way during the war

airplane spotters could identify
the stench from mountainsides
vapor trails, oil leaks, wings

and your fleecelined collar
still making its slow, wide turn
as if the rain stopped

and the river below
needs more sky – you come here
to climb until a map printed on cloth

unfolds inside each sleeve
spreads out – you still dry the jacket
on a few soft pages

from an old calendar, arms out
for some powerful dive, the chance
as if once it lifted the Earth and again.

•

This laundry basket half capsized
half motionless, breaking up
the way a raft will wait
till the wave in front settles down

– even Marieke knows how an audience
all at once and after the *Ladies*
and Gentlemen, for your...
and she's already giggling

watches how bluing is added
as if her eyes would never end
– she's already covered them
with empty towels, sheets

and tiny waves the sea can't hear yet
though she arrived minutes ago
"...*direct from performances before the...*
and the faint noise inside her eyes

– by now these wicker strands
are going off, fired and re-fired
non-stop applause and the stage
has something to do with boundaries

with little by little one foot
dances with the other
and this milky pillow case still warm
from all that salt in the water.

•

And your voice dissolves
circles slowly hour after hour
– you can tell this spoon

is more tired than usual
nodding back and forth
in front some carnival mirror

half aluminum, half fountain
half statue trying to wean itself
and your lips lopsided

as if more sugar
helps you forget why this spoon
knows the route

and once you ease it down
will sweeten the song
whose words you've forgotten

– it's past midnight
no one's here – the spoon
dipped to protect it

cover your mouth
as if it's you
who is singing that lullaby

over and over, over and over
the curtains drawn, the hum
struggling in armor.

•

Each night these branches lift off
dragging a tree
that is not a scarecrow

and though your jacket is unbuttoned
it flaps in the wind
to attract those birds

who believe leaves can migrate
once they learn more colors
– you invite the flutter

into these wide lapels
that need more feathers
for their descent, for the wings

each flock knows you grow
inside your sleeves
from water and darkness

– on both sides the sun's the same
just month after month
half thirst, half nightfalls

that aren't afraid anymore
when your shadow leans over the Earth
and drinks with its tiny eyelids open.

•

On tiptoe though this clock
adjusts for the approach
levels off the way a TV station

lets some tiger crouch
then crack your throat
– the flowers higher up

are blue but on the plains
mostly they're red
– you set this trap

on a wall that grows
out in the open
expects its hour hand

to protect you
though the soil is poor
once it leaves the valley

grows stones and snow
and footsteps: the numbers
never go off by themselves

each carries a list
– you were left behind
last wearing that jacket

torn at the collar, fleece
by the mouthfuls from counting
back and forth, airborne

exactly on the hour: each chime
circling you for a place to hide
as if it was being followed.

•

Half trough, half where this coral
stopped in front the way a horse
bends down without a rider

– it was a mistake, picking flowers
till your hand became a claw
learning how to swim sideways

though these tombstones by now
have grown over you
– there's no escape! one hand

arthritic, locked shut, no longer
waves out to sea and back
– a simple handshake smells from grass

and these reefs know how a greeting
is repeated till it seems natural
they bring tides here to spawn: this graveyard

must have lost its nerve
won't open any wider though your hand
is monstrous, a throwback, homesick

crawls cautiously toward a sea
little by little returning to rock
still slippery and the sun

who is not a beach remembers
and every evening leans over to drink
from the darkness and your lips.

•

Outside this graveyard wall: a sail
tormented by its sea – these waves
smelling from stone and the horizon

– a thin red line, faded
the way evenings unravel: all Earth
taking hold that single thread

rope walkers fit under the blindfold
and island to island – your fingers
stay put, lined up with the slab

coming by for more marble
give it curls, a name
and the same moonlight

even this motionless spider carries up
though the dead no longer trust
anything that flies – they remember

your umbrella, your handkerchief
and the first drop
suddenly appear on the sidewalk

to grasp your hand – your hand never dries
becomes some invisible stream
half crosswind hidden by seaweed

and wave after wave who long ago
lost their lips, are gasping for air
and each other – you reach out

careful not to slip, one arm
bent over, dangling, the other
left open, listens for wings.

●

There is no hallway: your casket
opens out so all that will enter
is already stone – your breath

has left for a sunlit attic
where it's more pleasant to wait
and your marrow once seawater

has hardened, is carried back
the way these flowers every Fall
become so heavy only you

can lift them from your mouth
breathe out the dim glare
from that first stone in the Earth

long enough – there is no door
that opens and closes and hovers
as if it still had wings

though every Spring more gravestones
that have their mother's eyes
can never stop grieving

– there is no chair, no rug, no wall
but the path goes wild
climbs out to look for you

in the shallows, in the rocks
in the broken waves year after year
and gather the sea together.

•

You read these notices, half bronze
half marble, half the slow, climbing turn
that has something to do with your arms

– they make a presentation, offer the dead
page after page: trees still standing
birdsong stuffed with newspaper and ponds

and after each frost
the almost invisible cracks
– there's barely room to kneel.

It happens every Spring, you wait
for the ice to overflow
loosen the darkness around all graves

– what you unfold is that fountain
continually leaving the Earth
to bring back these names where mourners

bathe their hands rotting in the open
and from your side the shadow
already going about its business.

●

One moon no longer thirsty, the other
caught by surprise – the splash
half glass, half rainbarrel

– that graceful neck you saw
lost the balance – not some sudden leaf
but it's easy to panic

not sure where the sky is – even stars
tremble on the water, drown
– I would have yelled up

not to trust your ears, they're filled
with crosswinds, throw you into turns
where your eyes are worthless

and there's no horizon, the sky
becomes the sea it once was
and moons, each looking for the other

the way I too was taught how rain
took on its raving hum – to fly
first, I learned it's called a ship

and even now the rain tightens clockwise
into some throat that has your feathers
even if dry and dyed – little friend

this time around you survived
but I drink only rainwater
collecting skies eaten through

patched, rotting on the ground
that has my eyes, the soft dirt
hiding my arms, mouthful after mouthful.

With fireworks it's easy but talk
isn't always a rekindled battle
– who knows why for hours
you'll whisper in a dark room
– even you think it's rain: words
have that softness at first, loosen
the way aerial gunners before each raid
still thumb through some songbook
pick out one, then end over end
and the page left open
tightening against the windowpane.

You stutter now, half feeble
half distant undersong, speak
as if your mouth clouded over
is falling out your throat
as these few hours when the rain
is stunning, shimmering across a silk shirt
opened over some beautiful woman whose thighs
fill up the house – you begin to undress
and though this room has nothing metal
what you breathe in is the descent
that follows every song around, waits
for you to forget a word, here, there
till your voice shuts down and the sky.

•

You dial as if one finger
would touch her hand and this time
open though the numbers and letters

must have had a simpler beginning
a time when arm in arm and even today
there is a Polarbear Club, swimmers

who have forgotten why they wait
for December, dancing in a circle
half Springsong, half under water

half some 13 year old – the splashing
must have been for some purpose
could be useful walking room to room

as if you were showing the house
to stones, thorns, the dirt almost radiant
and for the first time you say

how empty the sky is, talk into this phone
as if you were lifting something old
softly from her lips and the Earth.

•

This newspaper is still contagious
its obituary page torn out
but you never get it all – in weeks

a jaundice sets in, fever, slow tremors
and the attic dust already flickering
as if that page you use to start a fire

warms forever – those bodies are always cold
– it's only right you insulate
with something that will burn

lay down beside Esther's yellowed photograph
damp from the cellar – at this altitude
these rafters too are lowered into the place

made new again by just some chance
flames will come: arm over arm
one last pass, tighter, tighter

so the rope won't unravel in your hand
and the only return the dead remember
nothing but stones and open field.

You build the cake from a circle
already freezing over
– for mountainside

two candles, just one
and one to climb on
so nothing can grow tall

without you, not the small fires
on tiptoe, ready to fly off
– you almost bend one knee

for leverage, a gust
that could cool the Earth
lit by dust and rain

– you make a darkness, a deep breath
who step by step
approaches in a cone-shaped hat

– the cake you claim has your name
cast the way marble is sweetened
with shadows outlined on the ice

on the paper cups, the ribbons
nobody wants to wash
or keep or take in for the night.

●

One in the morning, louder and louder
completely naked, holding the phone
cold, motionless – in the dark

you sense you're not being heard
that one hand is smaller than the other
slower, frail, at two

you let go again, the lid
still slams as if your death
has not yet taken place

though another day has started out
alone, eating away at the cracks
at the dried-up handle

and near the bed a small cup for water
half empty, half covered
with a sail: the hillside

you had been keeping a secret
– it takes two mouths, one to yell
and the other drinks without knowing it.

●

You almost please, the pail
smothered the way sand
still expects a small red flame
and human sacrifice

– it's an old tradition, the shovel
held so one arm reaches slowly
to another though the dunes
have no trees left, are weighted down

by sunlight on this half-finished wall
– for more leverage you inhale
empty the Earth by patting the mound
till it crumbles stone by stone

already dried-out rain, evenings
half driftwood, half on fire
from your lips, your eyes
your hands and even now your breath.

•

They will carry off your eyes
the way ants are calmed by a darkness
that orbits the Earth – underground

a warm rain shape your skull
into the flower it once was
smelling from milk, from breasts

held close so you would remember
which petals were yours, which lips
which mountainside no longer thirst

and loneliness – they will take your eyes
single file, slowly in the dirt
that is not glue though you won't drink

from the rock that still has your forehead
hurtling down in rags already broken apart
for tears, for cheeks and at the bottom

always the three together, sending up
the hawk, the vines, the cliff
for its juices, its gentle leaves

its plumage that will feed piece by piece
even the sun, the stars, the your folded arms
shutting a door, a wall, a floor.

·

These clouds are never sure
climbing as if the sky is still mountainside
– will migrate till they're cold

then graze on snow, growing huge, dark
though when stars can't be found they sniff
for stones the way all trails are marked

break apart half ice, half some valley
falling toward evening – you can hear them
single file and even in sunlight

each drop takes on an unfamiliar shape
becomes the mourner who follows on foot
from darkness to darkness as snow

or thirst or an unknown distant path
with both sides holding on tight to you
to the still warm dirt, or nothing

– she's been dead for years
yet the rain stays frozen in this small stone
that splashes when your hands close over

tighter and tighter till it dangles motionless
and between your fingers and your lips
as if it could say something, tell you when.

•

When a seabird falls in love its heart
beats louder – you can hear the claws
and suddenly around your throat

from which there is no escape
though this cricket in back the couch
hides sometimes for hours

sometimes a whole day and slowly
a great distance closes in on you
– you hear how a gull

as if for the last time
circles down the way each grave
once in the ground

hooks on, can't be extracted
smells from stones and kisses
and little by little

your mouth begins to rattle
torn open, bleeding
from the shovel and the hunger.

•

Sometimes I forget to breathe, so what
– how much time does it take
to fall in love once this traffic light

turns red – I must have been eleven
or maybe younger, waiting for a girl's face
to pass behind the window pane

– I could see the moon, the table   .
the huge lampshade half red
half almost touching her hair

– today I had to push each breath in
with your legs, with your breasts
and the woman behind the cracked windshield

seated, looking around to this day
– even the dead need love and glass
isn't always rain though it's already Spring

and the car has begun to move
– only a second if I'm not looking
and people bump into me.

●

This attic has always sided with the bombers
leveled off and at exactly noon
you can hear the all-clear, begin

that slow climb to check for leaks
and though rain is no longer a single thread
there's still a trace, a tiny seam

broken open over a small cemetery
where through this shapeless hole
a young girl breathes in your face

wants to tell you something in secret
the way the sun still whispers
to the stones it left on Earth

– at this height your hand folds tenderly
around another till the silence
becomes shoreline still trying

twice each day to bring the sea
back up with it – 30,000 feet
half graveyard, half fuselage, half

before each flight you inspect the wooden crates
keepsakes and among the ruins two useless radios
both tuned to the same station

as if there's a difference in the weather
one step from another
when you bring flowers to remember

rain or no rain – you look around for winds
and the weeds need watering
though you press your face against the dirt

– what grows here are those stones
already clouds, almost in formation
and on her lips clinging to the ground.

•

The front door should be stone
so the room behind can lock
in one piece though Mahler

has to be sung by a woman
whose dress was torn away
on the dark corners, her breasts

sagging, sleepless, still nursing
her dead child while mourners
count the miles between each knock

and the next boundary line
– a woman's voice not yet those words
the dead still plant inside apples

cherries and higher in her throat
give birth to twins: the door
half facing left, half cut back

from mountainside, tormented
till it can return into the house
and out, freed from the ground

given feet and arms and wings
already grown, standing
naked in the doorway.

•

They still use bellows: your bare feet
sizzling the way a bird flickers through
bathed, fitted – from this puddle

each hoof already knows
how to rise, test the wings
folded tight around your ankles

– you stomp, heating this primordial ooze
till the waves lift your heels
that never forget their birthplace

come here after each rain
half feathers, half gallop
– it takes only minutes for the mud

to glow so you can grasp the sun
gently by the tip
though before it could fly

it pulled the Earth into the same fire
that smolders under you now
carries you up on a shoulder

side to side half stable
half daddy-ride, half sleeves
bent into stirrups, claws and your lips

already red from kisses, softened
could be used again to comfort
the bitter dust, its shadows and ashes.

•

It doesn't get any greener: doubt
takes on that shape all masks
have in common with horizons

– you're not sure these cars
are centered or the redeeming arch
will hover over the crosswalk

or crash as if nothing happened
or the trucks lined up in back
bloodsoaked from horns and yelling

– it's senseless to wait, the curb
is already curved, fits your cheeks
and ears and just as suddenly

will change again to red
– for those few minutes the Earth
dangles in the open, stained

while you stare at the emptied stoplight
filling it with stones and motionless Spring
– cemetery rows: the traffic

lasts forever though from the air
you can see a young woman
slowly walk toward you, bend down

with lips, kisses, breasts
– you lean against the wheel
become that stone whose genes

urge revenge, comfort the dead
– you wait for the grass that darkens
only as mountainside and footsteps.

•

The way a trawler will lift anchor
try further and further away
this lady at the MVB says come back

when your license expires
and then renew – it's not that important
I'm shorter or why the inch

is racing off without me
sucked into an immense yell
for more altitude – why can't she

just accept that moonlight
was never enough and give me a break
– as a woman she'll know

how to find my grave
but the stone will be confused
wants the claim in writing

up to the day that shows exactly
where in the ground the sun
was lowered for its first meal

and every day returns a piece
– it's just an inch but listen lady
I want it back, you had it last.

•

I can't breathe, the tub
half coffin, half rust
– once inside the shower

its fragile spray takes hold
tighter and tighter till the rain
can't wait: winds

are nothing new here
though I can break loose
untied, reborn, cleaned

the way this spider was paired
with the Earth, crawling closer
while the sun waits

stuck to the bottom
trapped by the black dot
it warms and escapes

only as morning, one strand
surrounded by dew
and the others.

．

How could something so soft
do any harm – naked, its waves
once stones falling from some mountainside

sweetened by streams: a sea made beautiful
more voluptuous than arm in arm
when huge sails would shape a song

sent back to shore as evenings a few hours
from the stars floating off
though an empty bottle could mean

the difference, would fill your hand
and no one begging for help – you would hear
this sea before its first tide: a pulse

a light being born, already weeping
– how can it be, this bloodstained sand
caressed the way waves

are still scented, made graceful
to welcome the lost, the splash
and because it is the thing to do

you cup your hands for tears
give back to the sea more stones
adrift, one colder than the other.